LIKE

ESSENTIAL POETS SERIES 252

**Canada Council
for the Arts** **Conseil des Arts
du Canada**

**ONTARIO ARTS COUNCIL
CONSEIL DES ARTS DE L'ONTARIO**

an Ontario government agency
un organisme du gouvernement de l'Ont

Canada

Guernica Editions Inc. acknowledges the support of the Canada Council
for the Arts and the Ontario Arts Council. The Ontario Arts Council
is an agency of the Government of Ontario.

We acknowledge the financial support of the Government of Canada.

Like

MAX LAYTON

**GUERNICA
EDITIONS**

TORONTO – BUFFALO – LANCASTER (U.K.)
2018

Michael Mirolla, editor
Cover and interior design: Errol F. Richardson
Cover artwork: Detail from *Androgyne*
by Betty Sutherland (aka Boschka)
Guernica Editions Inc.
1569 Heritage Way, Oakville, (ON), Canada L6M 2Z7
2250 Military Road, Tonawanda, N.Y. 14150-6000 U.S.A.
www.guernicaeditions.com
Distributors:
University of Toronto Press Distribution,
5201 Dufferin Street, Toronto (ON), Canada M3H 5T8
Gazelle Book Services, White Cross Mills
High Town, Lancaster LA1 4XS U.K.

First edition.
Printed in Canada.

Legal Deposit – First Quarter
Library of Congress Catalog Card Number: 2017955486
Library and Archives Canada Cataloguing in Publication
Layton, Max, 1946-, author
Like / Max Layton. -- First edition.
(Essential poets series ; 252)
Poems.
ISBN 978-1-77183-247-2 (softcover)
I. Title. II. Series: Essential poets series ; 252
PS8623.A9483L55 2018   C811'.6   C2017-906450-9

For my daughter, Jessica

TO SING ANOTHER VILLANELLE

To sing another villanelle
We climb or, drowning, die of thirst
At the bottom of this well

No fitter rhyme could this tale tell
For we, though last, are not the first
To sing another villanelle

When towers burned in sky-high hell
We found our world, ourselves, reversed
At the bottom of this well

When lovers jumped and others fell
Our parched hearts yearned, before they burst
To sing another villanelle

That sidewalk thump will sound our knell
Unless that sound, in art, is nursed
At the bottom of this well

Though words can never death dispel
Our spirits rise in verse unhearsed
To sing another villanelle
At the bottom of this well

Contents

I LIKE LIKE

I like like because it links
The most unlikely things

I like mice, for instance
Because they are like
Tiny elephants

And I like elephants
Because their ears
Are like butterfly wings
Opening and closing like
The eyelids of my first girlfriend

I remember the way she used to
Bump up against me like a whale
Surfacing from the deep

And the way we made love so
Effortlessly, like wind rippling
Through fields of summer grass

NOTHING LEFT TO SAY

Like a fish
In the shadows
Behind a rock
You swam away

Like a fox
In a field
Of sunburnt grass
You hid when I came close

Like a house
On a hill
In a landscape painting
I waited

Like a cat
By a door
In the rain
You scurried in

Like a TV
Left on all day
We had nothing
Left to say

AT THE HOME FOR HOMELESS POEMS

The first thing that hits you, when
You enter the shelter, is the smell
Of piss and disinfectant

Then it breaks your heart to see
So many abandoned poems

So many long rows of cages, noses
Pressed against the bars

I hold out a morsel of kibble hoping
A poem will lick my hand

Stray poems mostly, some obviously
Neglected for years

This poem missing an ear, this one
An eye, this one soon to be put down

Though some come from good lines
Most are indifferent and deformed

Frankly, I am amazed anyone cares
Enough about poems to protect them

Here, the attendant says, is a litter
Of newborn odes and a basket of
Unfinished villanelles

I peer inside and see an untidy heap
Of sonnets, limericks, elegies

In a corner, sleeping alone, a very
Rare epithalamium

The attendant opens the cage doors
And several lyrics tumble out

One of them, just a few months old
Comes hopping towards me on three
Legs

It is so eager for attention its whole
Body is quivering

I can't help myself and pick it up

The attendant says she loves them all
But admits this one is her favourite

She says she likes its spunk

I pat the poem, feel it nuzzling against
My neck, its soft, pink tongue tickling
My ear

There is nothing sweeter than a young
Poem's breath!

I'll take it, I say. How much?

The poem was free but the prosthetic
Leg would have cost a fortune

Anyhow, now when it runs at full speed
Nobody notices it's missing a foot

IN ANOTHER LIFE

In another life I might have worn leather stockings
          and a
Deerskin jacket with bedraggled fringes on my
          sleeves

In another life I might, mouth watering, have stalked
          this goose
And shot it with a flintlock rifle

Might, in my hunger, have dashed across this river's
          shallow
Moat and brained its nesting mate before she could
          fly away

Anyway, I would have got the eggs

In another life I might have pierced this goose with
          an arrow
Or slashed its air-sack with a blade made of obsidian

In another life I might have torn this creature limb
          from limb
And eaten it on the spot

Or tossed it, along with heated rocks, into a birch
          bark pot

But as it is, I am wearing blue jeans and Birkenstocks
        and my fridge is full

As it is, I am sitting on a log smoking a cigarette and
        thinking
About a lawsuit I may or may not win

The goose, apparently asleep beside me, is standing
        on one leg
With its head tucked behind its wing

I say apparently asleep because, when I shift my
        weight, the
Head swivels up and scans the world for enemies

I puff on my cigarette, move my arm very slowly

The bird relaxes, stares straight ahead at the river
I finish my cigarette and we both stare at the river

This goose and his mate have been coming here
        for years
Always nesting in more or less the same place

I'd like to think they know I am a friend and that, if
        attacked
A merciless, meat-eating ape would come to their
        defence

The goose puts his head back under his wing and I
        sit there guarding them

IN THE CAVE OF DREAMS

In my time, I was the bravest
Warrior of my tribe

In my mouth a recipe of bear fat
Blood and crushed red berries

I spit the mixture through a reed

When I pull my hand away, there's
The likeness of my crooked finger
The one I broke jumping the horns
Of a charging bull

Lord of lion, rhino, horse, gazelle
I stare at them, not them at me

Mine is the hand upon the wall
The face you never see

MY KINGDOM'S CREATURES

I like leaning on my porch watching
My kingdom's creatures

Birds in the trees, squirrels running
Along the ground, my two dogs, the
Black and white kitten I've released
Into the world for the very first time

I like the way she sits on a rock, just
Listening

The way she looks back at me, her
Eyes round and wide, the blue now
Turning green

The way she scampers to me when
The dogs bark at a passing car

The way, seeing a bird impossibly out
Of reach, she hunkers in the grass, her
Hind end twitching, before she springs

Then, exploding in a crazy figure eight
How she stops sideways with her back
Arched, her tail bristling

If there is a Great Mandala, a wheel
Churning at the end of life, I'd like to
Know what spectacular deed I must do

To come back as a black kitten with
Four pure white paws

CATS

I love my cats and give them all they want
To eat

Yet the minute they slip outside they turn
Into mass murderers

Hardly a week goes by I don't find a dead
Bird on my porch

A gift perhaps, a way of saying thank you
For that feeder in my backyard

One of my cats sits under it for hours
Waiting for manna to fall from heaven

The other day I rescued a chipmunk from
Her jaws

The terrified creature scampering to the
Top of my head

I could feel its feet clinging to my scalp
While, God-like, I knelt in my garden and
Let it go

I found it on my porch next morning, its
tiny miraculous toes splayed as wide as
The all-seeing sky

TURKEY VULTURES

Like ladies-in-waiting making
A curtain of their skirts

So, all morning, they have been
In my backyard tearing at a dead
Racoon

One going in to eat

While the other half dozen stand
In a circle, their backs turned

Wings touching
Shielding us

AT THE ROYAL ONTARIO MUSEUM

Interesting how, 240 million years ago
All the land in the world was a single
Continent called Pangaea

How, when the first dinosaurs were
Smaller than my dog and weighed about
Three chickens, the great mantle split
Like a cell dividing

My wife Sharon taking photographs, we
Observed life's increasing ferocity

Teeth the size of bananas
A femur as thick as a tree
Vertebrae bigger than a bath tub

Our own lemur brains growing larger
And capable of inventing weapons

Apparently, in another 240 million years
All the land in the world will become one
Continent again

And that, said Sharon, will make killing
Each other much easier

FOR FRANS

When I think of you, Frans
I think of a dead seal
On an east coast beach

Its flesh so putrid not even
My dogs would eat it

Likewise a jellyfish

When I think of you, Frans
I think of a jellyfish
Drying in the sun

A puddle of gelatinous puss
Its poisons leached

A gob of snot
Horked by the sea

AFTER THE STORM

I've lived here twenty years and never
Seen the like

A freezing rain that left a carapace of
Ice on cars and roofs and trees

On power lines snaking across the road

Five days without electricity
Splitting wood for the wood-burning stove

Eating by candlelight
Milk going bad in the fridge
No way to wash dishes

Reading by candlelight
About Puritans in 17th Century New England
How they survived what scientists now call
The Little Ice Age

Afterwards, I cross-country skied across a field
My poles tick-tocking to the top of a wide hill

Where I stood surveying the devastation

The kind of devastation dinosaurs must have
Seen when that meteor hit and the world went
Dark and froze

And I thought of those Pilgrims in New England
How they spent even the coldest Sabbath days
Sitting on benches in unheated meeting houses
Stomping their feet to keep warm

They say during the long hours of the sermon
The chattering of their teeth sounded like a
Field of crickets on a hot summer's day

APRÈS MOI, LE DÉLUGE

One of the great pleasures in this old man's
Life is watching the rain

Standing on my porch with a warm cup of
Coffee, smoking a cigarette

I know, I know … But at my age what difference
Does it make

Friends and people much younger than myself
Dropping like the rain all around me, dropping
Like flies

Btw, did you know that Beelzebub is Hebrew for
Lord of the Flies, a book I taught for 20 years and
Never grew tired of

Watching row upon row of innocent eyes grow
Wide as its meaning sank in – one of the many
Pleasures I used to have and now miss

So I smoke a cigarette and watch the rain flooding
The dirt road in front of my house, listen to its
Hammering against the roof

I see a flash of lightning and count the seconds
Before the thunder comes shaking the world like
One of those gods I wish I could believe in

Me thrilled to think this might be it, this might be
The final reckoning, the deluge Louis the Fifteenth
Wanted to miss

The idiot! I'd give my right arm and both my
Slowly dimming eyes to see the splendour of
His raiment in the midst of this black firmament

But the sky clears and returns to a blue more
Faded than the blue I remember as a kid

My wife pointing to flowers shattered by the
Rain, both of us shaking our heads, saying how
Beautiful our garden once was

BACK IN THE GOOD OLD DAYS

The trouble is we no longer know how
To make the simplest things

Things like a good eraser, the kind we
Had back in the good old days

Back in the good old days there was no
Mistake a good eraser couldn't fix

No lie you could not retell

Ex-wives, lovers, broken promises?
A flick of the wrist brushed them away

Indiscretions, embarrassments, stupidities?
The bits blew clean off the page

But now, no matter how vigorously I rub
There's always a dirty, grey, ever-widening
Smudge which nothing I do can change

Of course, I blame the Chinese
The crappy erasers they sell so cheap

Theirs is an ancient, subtle civilization
Which understands what torture a drop
Of water can be

The slow drip-drip of history

Those who cannot erase, cannot rewrite
Those who cannot rewrite, cannot create

Those who cannot create, will be erased

LAKSHMI

On the other hand, only a culture as
Ancient and subtle as India's could
Come up with Lakshmi, goddess of
Prosperity

The flat-screen TV, the matching fridge
And stove, dryer and washing machine

The car that doesn't come to a sudden
Shuddering halt in the middle of an L.A.
Freeway, leaving you marooned on the
Island of your mother's poverty

I was 15 at the time, visiting

I remember how, somehow, we pushed the
Car to the side of the road, then walked to
A restaurant parking lot where I sang until
We had enough money to call for help

I believe that was the first time Lakshmi
Spoke to me

She spoke again when I ran out of dough in
Israel and was forced to leave

She spoke when I worked in a factory

Most loud, most clear, she spoke when I owned
A bookstore in Toronto

When every night, at closing time, two or three
Of her best-looking avatars hung around, asking
Which Dostoyevsky novel they should read

Though older now, I am still tempted by Lakshmi's
Sensual laugh, her husky, voluptuous voice

When I open my iPad, the four arms of Lakshmi
Reach out for me

Behind the veil of illusion, the wheel of life
Turns like a Lazy Susan at the end of an
All-you-can-eat buffet

BELEVE®

Are you filled with emptiness? Do you
Wake up screaming in the middle of the
Night?

Do you spend hours tossing and turning
Worrying there's no purpose to your life?

Then you need Beleve®

Faster than a leap of faith, Beleve® is
guaranteed to cure your dis-ease

After just a few short weeks, the black
Hole at the centre of the universe will
Seem like the pupil of God's eye

Common side effects include hallucinations
And synaesthesia

Beleve® should not be taken in conjunction
With alcohol or marijuana

Abnormal behaviours such as staring skywards
While clasping hands together and falling on
Knees may be caused by Beleve®

Inappropriate hugging of co-workers without
Memory of the event has been reported

If you are bothered by life's most troubling
Questions, ask your doctor about Beleve®

THE OVERWHELMING

There are days when I cannot write a poem
So I understand the overwhelming emptiness

Understand why one of our proto-human
Ancestors went howling into the deepest
Recesses of his cave and started painting

Why so many since have felt the otherwise
Unlikely need to castrate themselves

Prostrate, castigate, flagellate themselves

And when even that was not enough:
Burn witches, be martyrs, kill infidels

Anything to hide the desperation behind the
Shining eyes of faith

Worse than the fear of God is the fear that
There is no god

Nothing out there except particles of dust
Swirling in the ruined halls of Heaven

WHEN YOU COME TO

When you come to, you realize you are
Trapped in a cage

Also, you notice you are wearing an orange
Jumpsuit soaked in gasoline

Thinking quickly, you rip off the jumpsuit
Because the floorboards are burning

You try climbing the upright iron bars but
Some bastard has greased them

That's when you hurl your body between
The bars and your head squeezes through

Turning sideways, you jam in your shoulders
And you laugh because the grease is helping

Next your chest

You squash it between the bars until your
Ribs pop

With one last desperate plunge, you burst
From the cage

And slide out between your mother's legs

MATTER OF TIME

The matter with time is
It's only a matter of time
Before all of us are fucked by fate

Like Betty Sutherland, my mother

Whose 15 years' worth of work
Went up in smoke in a fire in a
Gallery in Montreal

Who changed her name to Boschka
When she moved to the coast of
California

Where more of her paintings were
Tossed by a gust of wind into the sea

Little now to remember her by

A few last, best, scattered pieces

One of them the cover of this book

IT'S ITS SILENCE

It's its silence that scares me
And reminds me of my mother

The way, mouth open, she lay on the gurney
Before they wheeled her into the flames
And there was no scream

It's its silence that scares me
Like the last rose of summer

How still it still stands, pink and demure
While its petals unblossom and fall back to earth

Here, in this garden, where I've staked my ground
Time moves slowly but never slows down

MY FATHER IN WINTER

When I picture him, it is always
Summer and everything is green

So what is it about shovelling
Snow that makes me think of
Him?

Especially when my shovel cuts
Square blocks in knee-high drifts?

Why is it then I hear his voice
Saying what a good job I've done?

Perhaps, I think, my car is like a
Poem on a white rectangular page

But then I remember when I was
A kid

My father only some nights coming
Home

I remember working in the dark
In the middle of a Montreal winter

The snow deep and heavy

Me shovelling the driveway.
Making the edges straight

Waiting for his car to pull in

NEW DARK AGE

Looking back, if they look back at all
They'll say this was a new dark age

Bookstores shutting down
The collapse of the record industry

Not a single, intelligent, discussable
Movie being made

I remember the excitement we felt
Waiting for the next Fellini film

My father and the rest of us dissecting
Its meaning over endless cups of
Coffee at our favourite greasy spoon

And reading this, if they read at all
They'll be scratching their heads
Wondering what feeling excitement
Must have been like

SCARS

I have a scar on my right hand
I'd like to know how I got

Scars on my shins and knees
From hockey and falling off a
Bike

Scars from my parents splitting
Up

All these years later, the scars
Are still there

Though I've ignored and been
Bored by them

The scars are still there

Though I've worn and been torn
By them

The scars are still there

Inspect them, neglect them
Protect them, reject them

The scars are still there

RED SHIFT

There, that red you see is the anger
You so seldom express – resentment
Disguised as depression

I have no idea what the cause is

Perhaps your childhood and some
Experience with a previous lover

Also the discovery that you are not as
Talented as you used to think

The shell of your ego cracked like a
Cosmic egg

You seem to believe we are planets
Locked in permanent parallel orbit

Actually, that red shift you see is me
Moving away at accelerating speed

BEST I COULD DO

Thanks to the likes of you

Parents who loved their art more than
Anyone, including themselves

A woman who tricked me into fatherhood
Then marriage, then left

A friend who loved my second wife more
Than he cared for me

Thanks to the likes of you
Here is my novel
My book of short stories
My four CDs
This third book of poems

Under the circumstances
Best I could do

WHAT I LIKE ABOUT CANADA

What I like about Canada
Is what I like about my wife

Her vast, wild, natural beauty

I have swum in the lakes of her
Eyes

Pitched my tent in the crook
Of her arm

Portaged my canoe from vein to
Vein

Many times I have tramped up
The hill of a knee

And seen the winter drift of her
Snow-white skin

The continent of her summer smile

O Canada! Across your mountains
And your valleys I have journeyed

To all the far-off corners of my bed

FOR SHARON

If my desire could
Make it so

That tulip would stop
Bending in the wind

And this river would
Cease its flow

Clouds would stand still
And I would stand still

Staring at the blue
Of your eyes

At the sunlight flaming
In your red-gold hair

Ah wife!

I wish we could stay like this
Holding our breath forever

But then I remember
Your long graceful legs

The river flows
The tulip bends

IT BREAKS MY HEART

It breaks my heart to see my wife grow old
Those lips I kissed, that waist I liked to hold
Her hair now somehow traded, bought, swapped,
      sold
For silver where before was reddish gold

It breaks my heart to see her eyes grow dim
Light glinting on her reading glasses' rim
Her girlish laugh become a weary grin
Age a stain on her skin's enamelling

It even breaks my heart to have her near
To have her speak the words I ache to hear
That she will love me bald, while from my ears
And nostrils sprout more hairs than I have years

Yes, it breaks my heart to see much clearer
My own slow aging, her face my mirror

DEATH BUS

Of course I don't want to die but, if I must, I
Don't want to die in my sleep

I want a thrilling, mysterious death

One that leaves some seasoned detective drinking
Too much, the floor around his unslept-in bed
Strewn with mug shots and cigarette butts

I want him to admit that he's stumped, that he's
Never seen anything like it

I want my body washed for the autopsy

I want to see my blood draining, my ribs pried open
My heart held up to the light

I want the balding pathologist to notice, aside from
The bullet holes, the tiny punctures between my toes

I want him to shake his head at what I had for lunch

I want him to observe that I seem to have swallowed
A finger – perhaps my own

Though hard to tell since my hands are missing

Years later, I want my killer to kill herself, my dying

Words whispering in her head:

I see the death bus coming
It's shining in the sun
The good news is
There's room for everyone

EVIDENCE

The first thing he had to do was get rid of
The evidence

His computer, for instance

Even though all those searches for jihadi
Beheadings could be explained as curiosity

But how explain his interest in the anatomy
Of the neck?

That is why he now had a laptop

The trick was to have friends, go to work
Attend family dinners without expressing
A like or dislike about anything

To have no ideology, no motive, no reason to
Suddenly seize someone from behind and cut
His or her throat

That was his advantage

Especially if he did his work in winter and
Wore a hoodie and rubber gloves

And boots two sizes too big and deliberately
Left an imprint in the bloody, trampled snow

TV DINNER

If not me, then who is guilty of the
Suffering I see on TV?

It is as close as my remote:

The starving child with huge, brown eyes
Too weak to brush the flies away

The burned-out bus, the garbage-strewn
Streets, the dust

The legless beggar, the blind beggar, the
Empty cup

The bodies lying in neat, unlikely rows
The lines of refugees

The more suffering I see, the less I feel

The less I feel, the more my conscience
Bothers me

The more my conscience bothers me
The more I eat

AS SEEN ON TV

Are you constipated?

Some laxatives can cause cramps and
Sitting in a chair for long periods of time
Can leave you with a sore bottom

Fix plumber's butt and lose thirty pounds
Without dieting

Serious side effects include bleeding in
The brain, kidney failure, heart attack
And death

Order now and we'll double the offer

If mesh implants are eroding into your
Bladder, intestines or uterus, call for a
Free consultation

You'll like the way you look, I guarantee it

This year 3000 people will be diagnosed
With mesothelioma and any one of them
Could be a co-worker, a neighbour, a friend
Or a loved one

That's why I buy gold every chance I get

MRS. CANNIBAL

For every count, a countess
For every king, a queen

For every Napoleon, a Josephine
For every Hitler, an Eva Braun

For every Stalin, a Mrs. Stalin
For every cannibal, a Mrs. Cannibal

Likewise, for every slave-owner
A slave-owner's wife

For every capitalist pig, a capitalist sow

WEBCAM VIDEO

I hate to say I watched the scene
Two men framed in video screen

Sky of blue, hill of sand
Man in black, knife in hand

Man in orange, on his knees
Under sword of Damocles

Pagan, Christian, Atheist, Jew
Man in black hunting you

Man in orange, head held still
Man in black begins the kill

Man in orange, head held out
Man in black slits his throat

I'd like to say I looked away
The sad fact is I watched replay

JUST A HUNCH

Unlikely, but look at a map

Libya to Rome – 625 miles
Flight time – 2 hours

Load a plane with explosives

Fly it just above the waves
Into St. Peter's dome

Or the Sistine Chapel

Adam turned to painted dust
A hole where God had been

THE STERILE CRESCENT

In sculpture no likeness
In painting no people

In fashion no faces
In school no girls

In poetry no epic
In music no symphony
In drama no drama

No hero defying fate
No tragic inner flaw

No quest
No questioning

GROUND ZERO

Though they built a pool to cover it
Though they built a wall to keep us from it
We still fall into the pit

Though they built a pool to cover it
Our bodies fall where lovers sit

Though they built a pool to cover it
We drown in water's opposite

Though they built a wall to keep us from it
We still stare from towers' summit

Though they built a wall to keep us from it
When towers fall, we also plummet

Though the sidewalk does not split
We still fall into the pit

Though it stops us like a catcher's mitt
We still fall into the pit

ON TURNING SEVENTY

Me deking through a barbed-wire fence into
The maze that marks the river's edge

A chaos of vines and fallen trees walling off
The way ahead

Here, under the skirt of a towering evergreen
A winter's worth of scat which my dogs sniff at

Coyotes, probably
The fur of rabbits poking out

I am unafraid

Though no house around, no sound except
The river moving under ice

On the river's other side, a willow waiting
To be swept downstream

My dogs are waiting

They leap up eagerly when I turn and begin
The long trek back through the tangled wood

I am not lost

I have come to this place many times before
And I know exactly where I am going

SONG FOR LEONARD

Long green shadows
Sun slanting down
Wind in the leaves
I hear no sound

I'm lost in a thought
Not very profound

I'm lost in a thought
Where I'm frequently found

I sing for a friend
Who has turned to dust
I sing for him because I must

I sing for a god
That ought to exist
I sing to fill the emptiness

Yet, god or not
When I wake at night
I like the way stars
Are placed just right

The way the moon
So silently
Circles the world
And silences me

THE BIG PICTURE

I like getting lost in the woods
Especially in the fall when leaves
Cover everything

And all paths look the same

Not that, in the big picture, it makes
Much difference which path one takes

I like looking at the big picture

Especially in the fall when leaves
Cover everything

EMAILS

One thing I'd like to see
Is emails that self-delete

Best friend dead?
Erased without a trace

Not even an empty space
Where the name used to be

No stumbling across the
Deceased while scrolling
Through your address list

No need to be reminded
Suddenly, of your friend's
Non-existence

No need to face the need
To erase the name yourself

MY MP3 ME

My mp3 me
Deletes the unnecessary

The tinnitus
Like a plague of cicadas
In my head

The stupid things I've said

Still preserved, pristine
A winter landscape
A summer scene
Fall leaves, spring green

A few choice memories
Mom dad wife kids
A few extraordinarily beautiful women
One heartbreak, one recurring dream

My mp3 me is me
Without higher frequencies
Without infrequencies
Without mistakes
Fakes
Out takes

Things I never had or did
Things I hid

All of me
Mastered
Recorded

Ready to be sent
Uploaded

To the cloud

THE EYES HAVE IT

Found a blob of toothpaste
On my sweater

The one I wear every day

On the front, a few inches
Below the chin

Must have been there for
Ages

Since the last time I brushed
My teeth

Obviously, I don't look at my
Sweater as often as I should

I look at my greying beard
My thinning cheeks

Mostly I look at my eyes

I like to see if my eyes show
Signs of fear

Windows of the soul, they
Stare back at the crumbling
Edifice of my face

With pity and disdain

And then I feel much better

JUST GO ON LIVING

What is the likelihood, really, that
All of a sudden I might die?

Naturally, I was curious

So, I googled the government's
Actual actuarial tables

And discovered that I, a white male
Born in 1946, had a life expectancy
Of 64.4 years

I consider this pretty good news

Because it means I should have
Kicked the bucket five years ago

But here's where things get weird

According to these same statistics
If a man survives to age 70, his life
Expectancy shoots up to 83.7 years

Even more amazing, if a man lives
To 83, his life expectancy increases
To 89

And if a man lives to 89, he will live
To 93, and if he lives to 93, he will
Live to 96!

And so on

I know, I know what you're thinking
I thought the same thing myself

Socrates said all men are mortal
He even took poison to prove it

But statistics are statistics
Facts are facts

For every year you live, there's
Another year of life expectancy

My friends, I believe I have stumbled
Upon the secret key to immortality:

If you just go on living
You just go on living

ON THE ROAD

I'm listening to Beethoven
On my car radio
The second movement of
His Pathétique

So simple, peaceful, perfect

I'm in the express lane but
Traffic is almost at a standstill

Cars, vans, winter-dingy trucks

I am surrounded by thousands
Of people, all of us going very
Slowly wherever we have to go

I think there must have been
An accident up ahead

The sun is warm, smearing
Everything

A siren forces me to pull over
An ambulance flashes by

Tchaikovsky comes on
It's his Romeo and Juliet
The love troubles of the young

ME AND MY SHADOW

This trail I'm on must be aimed due
East

The sun, setting behind me, pushes
My shadow dead ahead

The lower the sun, the longer the
Shadow

Almost alien now: distorted head
On elongated neck

Arms, shoulders, legs impossibly
Ethereally thin

It strides in front of me as if trying
To get away from this old geezer's
Plodding steps

As if eager to plunge into the world
Darkening around me

So I stomp on its feet and keep it
Pinned down

Like my mother, me muttering under
My breath, "Not yet! Not yet!"

Except she was shouting, sitting bolt
Upright in bed, her heart stopped

Banging her chest with her fist, trying
To get it started again

THIS WALK

I like this walk which once, perhaps
Was an Iroquois track through woods
So thick not even a shaman could see
The railroad coming

The one that ran here for a hundred
Years past farmers' stump-cleared
Fields and the log tents they put up
Over square, stone-sided holes

All this, of course, before highways and
Trucks made the railroad obsolete

Now, the ties and rails torn out, I walk
My two dogs along this levelled path

I believe they like the fact it is always
The same path, though it changes with
The seasons – ice, sludge, flood, mud

How, at the moment, it is smooth and dry

I notice Fleck, the eldest, has been
Lagging behind this summer and no
Longer comes running when I call

I don't mind
I know the symptoms well

I use the time to yank a strangling vine
From an apple tree

Walk slowly among chokecherries and
Waterfalls of wild Canadian grapes

I have tasted them all and plucked poems
Here from the ancient air

In the far distance, the path bends and is
Screened by trees

Fleck is tired and I have no desire
To walk there either

CROSS COUNTRY

I broke trail yesterday, cross-country
Skiing through deep, deep snow that
Made a sunlit field a slanting plain of
Trackless white

All the way to the top of a hill where
The sky was

The view worth the blood pounding in
My head and the breath rasping in my
Lungs

I wrote a poem today, the lines breaking
Trail across the empty, field-like page

All the way to the bottom

OR YOU COULD SAY

Or you could say writing a poem is like
Shovelling snow on the Credit River

Same crisp white emptiness, same exposed
Lines of black, rock-solid ice

Except where the river insists on bubbling
Up and oozing over all your work

Where, when the spreading stops and
Smoothes and hardens, the skating is always
Best

This year I have shovelled rink enough for
Fifty kids

And a path snaking its way downriver until
It disappears around a bend

Fish staring upwards at this crazy old man
Prat-falling, flying across the ice

Frogs sleeping in the mud, crayfish huddling
Amongst the rocks – beaver, muskrat, mink

So much going on beneath the surface

OR NOT

If I live to be a hundred
Or not
I'd go on writing poems
Or not

What difference, at this point
Does it make

I'm too old to start a revolution
Or a new religion

Too stupid to invent something
Useful

Like a bullet that homes in on a
Heartbeat

But some day somebody will

No doubt the world is falling
Apart

No doubt we are going to Hell
In a handcart

Or a gas-guzzling car

I blame global warming for
Everything, don't you?

All these droughts and hurricanes
Refugees in the Middle East

Me wondering whether my poems
Will be preserved in Arabic

Or Russian
Or Chinese
Or not

IF IT WERE UP TO ME

If it were up to me, I'd write stronger
Longer-lasting poems

Hard to believe I worked as a logger
In northern B.C.

My thighs so thick they felt like
Limbs of trees

Hard to believe I picked tobacco in
Tillsonburg, Ontario

Callouses so thick I used them for
Stubbing cigarettes

Hard to believe I laid track from
Hudson Bay to The Pas, Manitoba

Afterwards, back in Montreal, I ran
All the way from Saint Catherine St.
To the top of the mountain

Then jogged around the freshwater
Lake formed by the crater of a spent
Volcano

Hard to believe I wasn't even out
Of breath

If it were up to me, I'd write stronger
Longer-lasting poems

Acknowledgements

I owe an incalculable debt of gratitude to my step-mother, Aviva, my friends Stephanie and Eamonn, and my wife, Sharon, for the hours they spent reading every line and whose many suggestions have improved at least some of these poems. Thanks, too, as always, to my friend Robert Priest for his inspiring example and to Leonard Cohen, whose teaching, encouragement, and advice is a loss not only to me but all of us. Finally, a heartfelt thank you to my mother, Boschka, a.k.a. Betty Sutherland, for painting *Androgyne*, a detail of which has been used for the cover. May these poems be worthy of her work!

"Après Moi Le Déluge" was previously published in *Freefall Magazine*.
"At The Home For Homeless Poems" was shortlisted for the Gwendolyn MacEwen Poetry Competition by *Exile Magazine*.

About The Author

Born in Montreal in 1946, the eldest son of poet Irving Layton and artist Betty Sutherland, aka Boschka, Max left home when he was 16 and survived by working as everything from tobacco picker, logger, and apprentice auto mechanic to vice president of a bank and high school English teacher. He is the author of a novel and a collection of short stories. As a singer/songwriter, he has produced four CDs, of which *True The North* is the most recent. *When The Rapture Comes* and *In The Garden Of I Am*, both published by Guernica Editions, are Max's previous books of poetry. For more information about Max, go to www.maxlayton.com.